Cover Photo

The National Martyrs' Memorial (aka Jatiyo Sriti Shoudho) is in Savar, Bangladesh. Construction of the monument was completed in 1982 and is a symbol in memory of the people who gave their lives in the Bangladesh Liberation War of 1971. In the center is the tallest pyramid, whose height is 150 meters. At its base contains the main mass of graves.

Hello boys and girls! Do you know how many countries are in the world today? The answer will depend a lot on how a "country" is defined. Some countries are members of the United Nations, others are not, and some are given only partial recognition. However, they are just as important to learn about. Which country do you live in?

My name is COUNTRY JUMPER, and I'd like you to come and jump with me around the world. I've selected 206 countries to visit, so put on your Jumping Shoes and buckle up. Today we are visiting **Bangladesh**, a country in the continent of Asia.

Table of Contents

Facts About Bangladesh

Tools connected to the Stone Ages dating back to over 20,000 years ago were discovered in the Greater Bengal region. Ancient Bengal was initially occupied by the Dravidians, Austroasiatics, Indo-Aryans, and Tibeto-Burmans. In the 3rd and 2nd centuries BC, Bengal was governed by the Mauryan Empire; however, the Gupta Empire eventually succeeded the Mauryan Empire in the 3rd century. A sovereign Bengal Sultanate was established by the 14th century and was later dismantled by the 16th century. It was invaded by the Sur Empire around 1532. Toward the end of the 16th century, the Mughal Empire conquered the Bengal delta after the Battle of Tukaroi. The Bengal Presidency was formed in 1765 after the rule of the British East India Company began. The British divided Bengal in 1905 and established the administrative division of Assam and Eastern Bengal. The Muslim League established

1

a parliamentary government in 1943. The victory of the Bengal Muslim League at the Indian provincial elections in 1946, set the course for the division of British India and the formation of the Dominion of Pakistan on August 14, 1947. Between 1947 and 1970, there was constant friction between East Bengal and the Dominion of Pakistan. During the nine months of the liberation war, Bengali locals proclaimed a declaration of independence on March 26, 1971. Dhaka is the capital of Bangladesh. The estimated population in mid-2019 was approximately 168,212,000.

The national flag of Bangladesh was designed by a student named Serajul Alam. It was last modified on January 13, 1972, and adopted on January 17, 1972. The red disc on top of a dark green, blue field is also featured on the Japanese flag. It is offset slightly toward the left side so that it appears centered when the flag is flying. The green represents the landscape of the country. The red color symbolism was defined as the bloodshed by Bengalis in their fight for independence during the Bangladesh Liberation War. However, the disc itself represents the rising sun of a new country.

Bangladesh's national emblem was adopted shortly after independence in 1971. A water lily is bordered on two sides by rice sheaves. Four stars and jute leaves are located above the lily. The water lily represents the rivers that flow throughout the country. Rice represents the staple food of Bangladesh, and for the agriculture of that nation. The four stars represent the founding principles in the current constitution of Bangladesh of 1972: nationalism, secularism, socialism, and democracy.

A country's coat of arms (emblem) is a symbol that signifies an independent state in the form of a heraldic achievement. An important use for national coats of arms is as the main symbol on the cover of passports.

Over 98 percent of the people in Bangladesh speak Bengali, which belongs to the Indo-Aryan group of languages and is related to Sanskrit. It contains many words from Portuguese, English, Arabic, Persian, and Hindi. Dialects of Bengali are spoken in some parts of the country, which include non-standard dialects such as Chatgaiya, Sylheti and Rangpuri, and Pakistani Biharis. Several indigenous minority languages are also spoken as well as English.

Islam is the official religion of Bangladesh. It is practiced by around 88 percent of the country's population. Bangladesh is home to the second-largest ethnic group of Bengali Muslims in the Muslim world. It has the fourth-largest Muslim population in the world and is the third-largest Muslim-majority country. Most Bangladeshi Muslims are Sunni, followed by Shia, and Ahmadiya. Minority religions include Hindu, Buddhism, and Christianity. Around four percent of the residents are non-denominational.

Baitul Mukarram National Mosque
ID 187393352 © Matyas Rehak | Dreamstime.com

Terrain and Climate of Bangladesh

The terrain of Bangladesh has two distinct features, where it is mostly flat in the plain and hilly in the northeast and southeast. The broad deltaic plain is subject to frequent flooding, and the small hilly region has swiftly flowing rivers. Its climate is tropical with a mild winter from October to March, and a hot, humid summer from March to June. Natural disasters, such as cyclones, floods, tidal waves, and tornadoes, occur almost yearly. Bangladesh has six seasons divided as follows: summer, monsoon, autumn, late autumn, winter, and spring.

Politics of Bangladesh

Bangladesh practices a parliamentary democracy where the electorate elects representatives who then chooses a ceremonial president. It operates under the framework of a multi-party system. The head of state is the president, and the head of government is the prime minister, who is invited by the president to form a government every five years. A key aspect of politics in Bangladesh is the "spirit of the liberation war," which refers to the liberation movement's ideals.

Residence of the President
Image by Aminul Joy@ https://com-mons.wikimedia.org/w/index.php?curid=72373337

Education in Bangladesh

Bangladesh has expanded access to education over the last decade, and it now has one of the largest educational systems in the world. The government operates many schools at the primary, secondary, and higher secondary levels, and subsidizes many private schools. Primary and secondary education are both compulsory and lasts for 12 years. Primary consists of eight years, while secondary lasts four years. Secondary education is divided into a lower level and a higher level.

University of Dhaka
Image by Salim_Khandoker @ https:// commons.wikimedia.org/w/index.php?curid=70933099

Transportation in Bangladesh

In Bangladesh, transportation is a vital part of the economy. Buses, planes, rickshaws, auto-rickshaws, taxis, and trains are the primary means of transportation. Auto-rickshaw is an environmentally-friendly form of transport because it uses compressed natural gas as fuel. There is also the tuk-tuk, which is basically like a three-wheeled go-cart. Bangladesh has 1,681-miles of rail network, and 5,000 miles of navigable waters, one of the largest inland waterway networks globally. There are three international airports in the country.

Rickshaw

Holidays and Festivals in Bangladesh

Victory Day in Bangladesh is always celebrated on December 16. It is also called Bijôy Dibôs when translated in Bengali. The holiday commemorates the victory of the allied forces over the Pakistani forces in the Bangladesh Liberation War in 1971. The holiday begins with a 31-gun salute at the National Parade Ground at Sher-e-Bangla Nagar, followed by a military parade, ceremonial meetings, speeches, lectures, receptions, and fireworks.

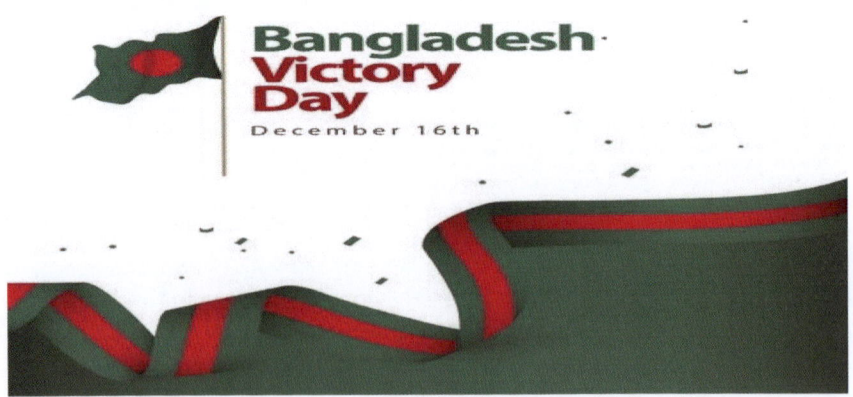

ID 141065421 © Ahmad Tobroni | Dreamstime.com

Pawhela Boishakh (New Year's Day) is the first day of the Bengali calendar. It is the most renowned secular national festivities in Bangladesh, and it is celebrated on April 14 as a national holiday. Boshakhi fairs are one of the highlights of the day, where there are huge amounts of various food, dancing, handicrafts, toys, music, and much more. Pawhela Boishakh is also marked by a wide variety of cultural shows, processions, family time, and other programs. People eat sweets, dress up in kurtas or saris, and wish everyone a joyous new beginning.

Animal, Bird, Flower of Bangladesh

The national animal of Bangladesh is the Royal Bengal tiger. This tiger is considered to be a powerful, intelligent, and majestic animal. Their stripes pattern is unique to each tiger. Its primary habitat includes forests, grasslands, mangroves, and vegetation. They are avid hunters of both small and large mammals, and they can imitate the sounds of other animals to lure their prey. One of the largest wild cats alive today is the Bengal tiger; however, they are currently threatened by poaching and loss of habitat.

Image by Free-Photos from Pixabay

The magpie robin is the national bird of Bangladesh. It is displayed on the country's currency notes and is a common sight throughout Bangladesh. These are medium-sized birds commonly found in forests and urban gardens. The male's upper part, throat, and breast are shiny blue-black in color, while the female instead has a brown-grey color. These birds are especially well-known for their songs and were once popular as cage birds. They have a collection of melodic calls and are notorious for imitating other bird calls. The Seychelles magpie-robin is one of the most endangered birds in the world.

ID 123166527 © David Havel | Dreamstime.com

The shapla (waterlily) is the national flower of Bangladesh. There are approximately 70 different species of waterlilies around the world. They are tuberous and are rooted in soil in bodies of water, such as lakes, ponds, and wetlands, with leaves and flowers floating on the water surface. Flowers from the waterlily opens during the day and closes at night, others open and close in reverse order. The waterlily's tubers and rhizomes can be used as food items that are often boiled or roasted.

Popular Foods
of Bangladesh

A national fish dish in Afghanistan is ilish macher dhakai paturi. Ilish is a fish, and this dish involves the fish being wrapped in a banana leaf and baked, steamed, or fried. The fish is marinated with ground spices, and mustard seed paste; grated coconut, and eggplant are also added. Mustard seed has a very pungent flavor, and when combined with the banana leaf, they both compliment the taste of the fish. The banana leaf is very delicate, so wrapping the fish is a little bit tricky.

ID 29755575 © Nilanjan Bhattacharya | Dreamstime.com

The pitha is a type of rice cake that can be made at any time of the year; however, it is strongly associated with harvest festivals in Bangladesh. Pithas can be eaten at small meals, such as breakfast or as a snack with tea. The most common ingredients are unboiled rice or wheat flour, molasses or sugar, coconut, and oil. It is then fried in oil, slow-roasted over a fire, steamed, or baked and rolled over a hot plate. Pithas can also be prepared with stuffed vegetables inside of them.

কাঠিপিপঁড়ে @ https://commons.wikimedia.org/w/index.php?curid=65979003

Mishti doi is a traditional sweet treat in Bangladesh that has a rich taste of sweetened yogurt. It is made primarily with milk, caramelized sugar, and plain yogurt. During preparation, the milk is boiled until it is slightly thickened and then sweetened with sugar. It is often seasoned with a pinch of cardamom for fragrance. An earthen bowl or pan is ideal for preparing mishit doi in because the earthen bowl absorbs the moisture from the doi, which makes it thick. This mild and light treat makes a great dessert option when entertaining guests.

Money in Bangladesh

The Bangladeshi taka (Code: BDT) is the currency of Bangladesh. The taka was introduced in 1971 after Bangladesh gained its independence from Pakistan. It replaced the Pakistan rupee. The word taka is commonly used by the locals to describe any money currency. Banknotes currently in circulation are the 5, 10, 20, 50, 100, 500, and 1,000 takas. Coins in circulation are 1, 2, and 5 takas. The 1-taka coin is rare and is seldom used.

ID 98373924 © Sayda Nargish Parvin | Dreamstime.com

Sports in
Bangladesh

The national sport of Bangladesh is kabaddi, a contact team sport originating from India. A single player on offense runs into the opposing team's half-court, and tag out as many of their defenders as possible. The player has to return to his own court without being tackled by the defenders. However, one of the most popular sport in Bangladesh is cricket, followed by football (soccer). Other popular sports include angling, badminton, basketball, chess, field hockey, handball, shooting, tennis, and volleyball.

Music and Instruments of Bangladesh

The music of Bangladesh features the Baul mystical tradition that celebrates spiritual love. The music involves songwriting that spans over a period of almost a millennium. Bangladeshi music documented the lives of the people and was widely utilized by the rulers. A one-stringed instrument known as an ektara is used in folk music. The ektara is a drone lute with a gourd resonator that is covered with skin, through which a bamboo neck is inserted. Other popular instruments include the dotara, dhol, flute, and tabla.

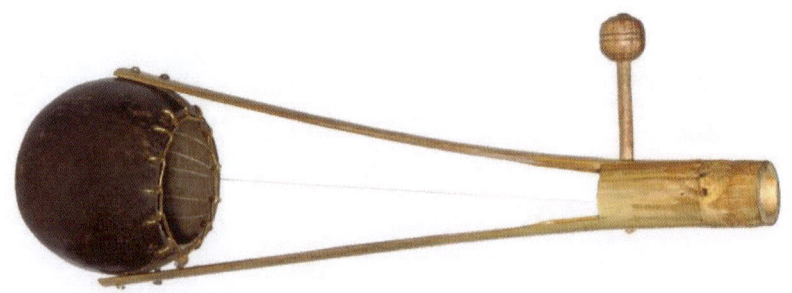

Ektara

Clothing in Bangladesh

The kurta and sherwani are the national clothing of Bangladeshi men. The lungi and dhoti are worn in informal settings, and there is also traditional wear called Panjabi, worn during cultural and religious events. The sari is the national dress for Bangladeshi women; however, the shalwar kameez is also commonly worn. Bangladeshi women also purchase Burmese floral fabrics to have a tailor make their outfits.

Sherwani

Fun Places for Kids to Visit in Bangladesh

Fantasy Kingdom in Bangladesh was opened on February 19, 2002. It is the only theme park in the country. Popular rides include Magic Carpet, Roller Coaster, Giant Splash, Slide World, Wave Pool, Tube Slides, Ferris Wheel, Paddle Boat, and much more. There is also amazing landscaping with dinosaurs, rock gardens, and bubble pools. Prince Ashu, Princess Lia, and their animal friends Zuzu, Bobo Zipper, and Bangasaur are always at the park welcoming visitors with a smile.

The Bangladesh National Zoo is the largest in the country. The zoo has around 165 species of animals, with around 2,000 of them on exhibit. These include baboons, Bengal tigers, black bears, cheetahs, chimpanzees, deer, elephants, giraffes, hippos, hyenas, impala, lions, otters, rhinos, tapirs, waterbucks, zebras, and lots of monkeys. Other attractions and activities at the zoo include a museum, aquarium, elephant and horseback riding, and fishing.

Image by Niriho khoka @ https://commons.wikimedia.org/w/index.php?curid=49406421

Bangladesh Air Force Museum is one of the best aviation museums in this world. It was created to retain the history, success, and development of the Bangladesh Air Force for future generations. The four galleries include the Air Force gallery with memorable and historical photos, the Liberation War gallery depicting the history of this war, a gallery displaying medals and uniforms, and the peacekeeper's corner. There is also a park just for children.

Other Interesting Facts About Bangladesh

- ❖ The national Parliament of Bangladesh is one of the largest legislative centers, occupying 200 acres of land.
- ❖ Bazar Beach is 75 miles long and is one of the longest beaches in the world.
- ❖ Bangladesh has the world's largest river and the world's largest mangrove.
- ❖ Bangladesh is one of the most disaster-prone areas in the world. Cyclones and floods have killed thousands and impeded economic growth.
- ❖ More than half of Bangladesh's population is composed of farmers.
- ❖ Females in rural areas are not required to attend school.
- ❖ In Bangladesh, the left hand is considered unclean, so always use your right hand when eating or passing food, drinks, or business cards.
- ❖ The people of Bangladesh seldom smile, because smiling much is considered a sign of immaturity.
- ❖ In 2016, Bangladesh Central Bank was the target of a massive bank heist. Hackers attempted to steal US$1 billion, the biggest heist in history.
- ❖ Its national fruit is the jackfruit.
- ❖ Traffic is insane.

Barbados is the next stop on our journey. Are you ready to soak up some island sun? The travel distance between Bangladesh and **Barbados** is 9,186 miles. It will take around 16.4 hours to get there by plane.

REFERENCES

1. http://www.studycountry.com/guide/BD-history.htm
2. https://en.wikipedia.org/wiki/Bangladesh
3. www.worldometers.info/world-population/bangladesh-population/
4. https://omniglot.com/language/phrases/bengali.php
5. https://en.wikipedia.org/wiki/Victory_day_of_Bangladesh
6. https://einfon.com/nationalsymbols/national-animal-of-bangladesh/
7. https://www.sunderbannationalpark.in/blog/amazing-facts-about-royal-bengal-tiger/
8. https://www.bangladesh.com/blog/the-fascinating-oriental-magpie-robin/
9. http://www.mellownspicy.com/2014/10/03/ilish-macher-paturi-pan-fried-hilsa-in-banana-leaf-cooking/
10. http://weloveourbangladesh.blogspot.com/p/pithas-are-part-of-food-tradition-and.html
11. https://www.vegrecipesofindia.com/mishti-doi-recipe/
12. https://www.fantasy-kingdom.net.bd/
13. https://bnzoo.org/
14. http://offroadbangladesh.com/places/air-force-museum/
15. http://srune.com/lists/40-facts-about-bangladesh/74
16. http://nationfacts.net/bangladesh-facts/
17. https://www.worldatlas.com/articles/fun-facts-about-bangladesh.html
18. https://www.distancefromto.net/distance-from-barbados-to-bangladesh
19. https://www.onceinalifetimejourney.com/inspiration/interesting-facts-about-bangladesh/

Continue following *COUNTRY JUMPER* as he treks across the globe from countries A through Z. Why stop here when there is so much more to learn about this great big world? Where will the next jump take you? You can follow *COUNTRY JUMPER* on his journey from A through Z or jump into the countries that you are curious to learn more about. A total of 206 books representing each country will be available in this series. If you cannot find a country that you would like to explore, please contact the author.

Happy reading!

Printed in Great Britain
by Amazon

11634101R00020